# The Second
# American
# REVOLUTION

# The Second
# American
# REVOLUTION

## SECOND EDITION

Gerald McIsaac

ISBN: 978-1-952302-82-4 (hc)
ISBN: 978-1-952302-83-1 (sc)
ISBN: 978-1-952302-84-8 (e)

Library of Congress Control Number: 2021920373

# PREFACE

As I write this, the Covid 19 virus is raging out of control. The current American death toll, as a result of the virus, is approaching 270,000 and is expected to *double* within the next couple of months. The press, or at least all the major mainstream news networks, have quite gleefully reported that the federal election is over, Trump has lost, Biden is now the "president elect", and Trump should "quit playing golf and prepare to spend the remainder of his 'golden years' in a 'correctional institution'."

Perhaps the journalists are blinded by their hatred of Trump. The man is by no means the "sharpest tool in the shed", but nor is he entirely stupid. He has hired a rather impressive team of lawyers, including experts on constitutional law, and those "legal eagles" are almost certainly telling Trump precisely what he wants to hear. Strangely enough, it may even be the truth. The fact is that the Twelfth Amendment to the Constitution makes no mention of the popular vote. It is the *Electors* who vote for the President, as well as the Vice President, and not the American voters. Further, those same lawyers are prepared to argue, before the Supreme Court, that the states have no right to meddle in a federal election. This is to say that any state laws which place restrictions on the Electors are not constitutional. If the Supreme Court agrees, then the current two-party system will effectively be abolished.

The fact remains that the Electors are about to vote, on December 14. Those votes will then be placed in sealed envelopes and sent to Washington, before December 23. Then on January 6, in front of the joint session of the Senate and House of Representatives, the President of the Senate, who is also the Vice President, will open each envelope and read aloud the names of the persons nominated for President and Vice President. The individuals who receive 270 votes will be the next President and Vice President, respectively. If no candidate receives the required majority, then the matter goes to the House of Representatives.

It is significant that the lawyers who work for Trump have been advising the state legislatures to nominate Electors who will vote for Trump, or at least anyone but Biden. They are advising the newly appointed Electors the same thing.

Assuming the Electors listen, many of them could end up voting for the former First Lady, or Senator Sanders, or even Senator Harris for President. The Electors refer to this as "voting their conscience", and is quite possible, if not likely. Assuming that happens, it will result in a proper "gong show", to put it in popular terms.

Lately the revolutionary motion has experienced a lull, at least here in North America. Yet we can expect it to rise up "with a vengeance", especially if Trump is re-elected. This motion is unprecedented in its scope and magnitude. We can expect it to erupt in full scale revolution, and very soon.

Never before has a revolutionary motion on this scale been seen. What is more, it is being *led by women!* The discipline and dedication of these ladies are to be admired. The only thing lacking now is direction, as the uprising lacks focus. The goal of this revolutionary uprising must be scientific socialism, in the form of the Dictatorship Of the Proletariat. That is the one -and only- alternative to capitalism.

The recent protests, which have mainly been led by women and include Black Lives Matter, have been largely peaceful. The people who are taking part in this revolutionary motion are now coming together, spontaneously gravitating towards socialism. One of the most encouraging posters read:

# TRUMP IS THE SYMPTOM

# CAPITALISM IS THE DISEASE

# SOCIALISM IS THE CURE

This is absolutely correct, but as yet contains no class content. It is certainly a step in the right direction.

No doubt the revolutionary uprising has inspired a great many people to become politically active. Those who were formerly apathetic are now rising up, burning with passionate indignation. Welcome, my Brothers and Sisters, my Comrades! It is for your sake that I will explain a few basic facts, which have been hidden from you. The capitalists do not want us to be aware of any of this! Yet it is vitally important that all working people become familiar with certain scientific terms, so bear with me.

We live under a state of monopoly capitalism, referred to as imperialism, which is complete reaction. This is to say that there in nothing progressive about the capitalists. The monopoly capitalists, the billionaires, comprise a class of people who are technically referred to as the bourgeoisie. There are very few of them, or they are "numerically small", to use the correct technical term, perhaps a few hundred. Yet they are the class of people who rule the country. They own the "means of production", which is to say the mills, factories and mines, as well as the railroads, airlines, internet and all communications companies. They perform no useful service, merely "invest their capital" and demand a proper "rate of return" on that capital. This is to say that they "skim the cream" from any businesses they own.

This means that they force their workers to labour as hard as possible, while paying them as little as possible. It also means that as "reactionaries", they are determined that nothing will change. That includes the schools. The history and science books are to remain the way they are. That which is written is to remain written. They run the schools the same way they run the country. "No change" is a recipe for disaster.

This is completely unacceptable. The classes are always in conflict, but soon that conflict will break out into open warfare. The working class, the proletariat, is rising up and challenging the rule of the capitalists, the bourgeoisie. It is necessary to overthrow that class of parasites and crush them, to exercise dictatorship over them, the Dictatorship Of the Proletariat.

With that in mind, it is necessary to challenge them wherever they are, including their golf courses, homes, places of business, resorts and universities. We must give them no peace, as this is class warfare, so that the enemy must be given no chance to regroup and counter attack.

The capitalists have not only crushed and exploited us. They have also robbed us of our heritage and our history. It is in the interest of restoring to the working class, that which is rightfully ours, that I have written this book.

For many years I have been looking into the existence of numerous species of huge animals, which the scientists insist are extinct. In fact they are very much alive, and as such, are part of our heritage. As well, our history books are filled with distortions and outright lies. These must be corrected, as we are also entitled to our history.

It is encouraging that the members of the public no longer refer to the billionaires as the "1 percent", just as they no longer refer to themselves as the "99 percent". No doubt there is a growing awareness that the billionaires are far fewer that one in a hundred, and closer to one in a million. It is clear that the level of awareness of the working class is growing. Now it is necessary to build upon that awareness.

I am well aware that the scientists are successful, well educated and well respected. I am also convinced that they are well aware of the existence of these animals and choose to deny it. That is supremely hypocritical and equally stupid.

That is a strong accusation but consider the facts. The pterosaurs are flying reptiles, predators with a wing span of ten to fifteen meters, or thirty five to fifty feet. They prey upon people as well as livestock. The disappearance of so many women and children is cause for great concern. As well, the mutilated carcasses of cattle and horses have baffled all investigators. Yet the culprit is these flying reptiles, and still the scientists insist they are extinct. As if an animal that size can be kept secret!

In addition, the scientists continue to claim the extinction of the largest land dwelling animal in the world, the woolly mammoth. Also the largest bear in the world, the short faced bear. The largest canine, the dire wolf, even though they admit it still exists! Then there is the Jefferson ground sloth, named after the third American president. Lest we forget, the huge cat within the city of Milwaukee, referred to as the Milwaukee Lion, is in fact a sabre toothed cat.

There are others, most notably gigantopithecus, commonly referred to as Sasquatch or Bigfoot. It is in fact an ape, twice the size of gorillas and a separate species of human. I refer to them as Giants. Of course, there are others, yet the scientists think that they can keep their existence a secret!

It may be objected that the scientists are in the service of the bourgeoisie, and to even suggest the existence of these huge species is to commit career suicide. That is no doubt true, but it in no way changes the fact of their hypocrisy. The search for these "prehistoric" species is referred to as *cryptozoology*, which means "the quest for animals that the scientists claim to be extinct". The scientists tend to refer to this as "crazy zoology". Let it never be said that the scientists do not have a sense of humour! That is a good thing, as they are going to need it when we prove these animals still exist.

Lately, Skinwalker Ranch in Utah has been in the news. Apparently, they have been plagued with the death of livestock. Those animals are being found dead and mutilated in the morning. As there is no blood around the wound sites, people assume that the blood has been drained. Also, the wounds are specific to the genitals, face and the large intestine ripped out. The explanations being put forward are nothing less than an embarrassment.

The most ridiculous suggestion is that Extra Terrestrials are responsible for this killing. As proof, the appearance of lights in the night sky is offered. These are commonly referred to as UFO's, perhaps the glow from spacecraft. As well, the dire wolf has been seen, a wolf the scientists assure us is extinct, even though they admit that it still exists. Just as the "Sasquatch", or Giants, have been spotted. This calls for a proper scientific explanation.

The fact is that in the darkness, the pterosaurs, or pterodactyls, fly in and release a "cloud of smoke", as it is commonly called, which is in fact toxic, poison gas. This kills the animals so that the heart quits beating. As every school child knows, once the heart quits beating, any wounds that are inflicted do not bleed. That is the reason there is no blood around the wound sites.

Then the predators feast upon the items they can easily access, which include the genitals, the face and large intestine. As the animals weigh a mere thirty pounds or so, they are not capable of tearing apart the carcass.

The simplest, easiest way to prove the existence of these animals, is to draw out a sample of blood, from the carcass of an animal which has recently been killed, and send it to the lab. The lab will in turn determine the poison gas which was used to kill them. Also, swab around the wound sites and send those swabs to the lab, in order to determine the DNA of the animal which inflicted those wounds. Better yet, send samples to three labs, as the results will be challenged. When the DNA test result comes back as that of a reptile, there will no doubt be an uproar, as the cry goes up that there are no crocodiles in Utah!

That is true, but then it is not a crocodile that inflicted those wounds. They are being killed by pterosaurs, reptiles which are nocturnal, so that they avoid the light. They spend the day light hours inside caves in the mountains. No doubt the Indigenous Elders know precisely the location of those caves. If they are readily accessible, then cameras can be placed, in order to prove their existence. If not readily available, then there is a nesting site close to the village in which I live.

The Ranch also reports the existence of dire wolves, which the scientists have classified as extinct. It is also true that the scientists admit the dire wolves still exist. They refer to them as a "remnant population of an extinct species". I refer to this as an outright lie, pure hogwash. Those wolves are top predators, so they are also top scavengers. Two sides of the same coin. Of course such a bonanza is sure to attract them.

That brings us to Sasquatch, or Giants as I refer to them, which are also top predators.They too are drawn to that feast of hundreds of pounds of high quality meat.

As for the lights in the night sky, no doubt that is due to the fact that among the pterosaurs, the males glow during mating season, probably in April, as a means of impressing the females.

# CHAPTER 1

# THE FIRST AMERICAN REVOLUTION

The industrial revolution first appeared in Great Britain between 1720 and 1740. The resulting changes in society were immediate and dramatic. Of that there can be no doubt. Articles which were formerly made by hand are now mass produced. This revolution has spread around the world, and in fact is still spreading.

At that time, in Britain, the class of people whom were known as burghers saw an opportunity to become quite wealthy, and invested their money, or capital, in factories, mills and mines, among other things. They succeeded, beyond their wildest dreams, and became transformed into members of a different class, a class of capitalists, technically referred to as bourgeois, from the word burgher. Since that time, the "small time capitalists", or small business owners, are referred to as middle class, or petty bourgeois, while the "super rich", or billionaires, are referred to as the bourgeoisie. These are a few of the terms with which the working class must become familiar.

That brings us to the second class which was created, the working class, or proletarians. A proletarian has nothing to sell but his labour power. In scientific terms, we say that no class can exist in isolation, that a class can only exist with its "antipode", the class opposite to it. The bourgeois can exist only with the proletarian, and the proletarian can exist only with the bourgeois. Which is not to say that we are "bosom buddies", because we are not. In fact, from the moment the two classes came into existence, it was war!

The reason for this is quite simple. It is in the interest of the capitalist to force the workers to work as hard as possible, while paying them as little as possible. This ensures the maximum profit, that which they refer to as their "bottom line". The profit is the one and only reason they are in business.

To return to the time of the industrial revolution, the newly minted capitalists in Britain considered it best to restrict industrial development to the motherland, and have the colonies graciously supply the mills with the raw materials needed to produce the finished goods. In other words, it was in the interest of the British capitalists to have the colonies send their cotton, wool, hides and timber, among other things, so that the mills in Britain could process it into clothing, shoes and timbers, for example, and then sell the "finished product" to all and sundry, including the colonies. They considered this to the very "pink of fairness".

Not everyone was so enthusiastic concerning the idea of furthering the enrichment of the British capitalists. In particular, within the American colonies there was a "colonial aristocracy", a mixed assortment of burghers, in the north, and slave owners, in the south. The members of these two classes had only one thing in common: they considered the British bourgeois, as well as the nobility, to be the enemy.

The American colonial burghers wanted to follow in the footsteps of their British counterparts, to invest their capital in industry, to also build mills and factories, for example. The British capitalists saw this as competition, and took a "dim view" of this. In fact, there is nothing the capitalists hate more than competition. It cuts into their profits. With that in mind, industrial development in the colonies was strictly forbidden.

The southern American colonial slave owners were also concerned. The industrial revolution gave birth to capitalism, and capitalism creates a class of proletarians, while it leads to the destruction of other classes. This includes the class of slave owners.

In fact, the British government was taking steps to abolish slavery through out the empire. The southern colonial slave owners could see the "writing on the wall", knew that their "days were numbered". It occurred to them that it may be in their best interest to separate from the British, before the British separated them from their slaves. Hence the unusual alliance of northern capitalists and southern slave owners.

This led to the colonial rebellion of 1776, the American Revolutionary War, or the Colonial War of Treason, from the British perspective. It all depends upon your view point.

It is to the credit of the American revolutionaries that they took advantage of the antagonisms between the various empires, that of the British, French and Spanish. All three empires were fighting over the American continent, with each empire staking out a claim. In particular, the Americans appealed to the French, and the French responded with considerable assistance. They were only too happy to create as much difficulty as possible for their British enemies.

As the American revolution was successful, there is a lesson we can all learn. First there was an alliance of two classes, the capitalists and the slave owners. The only thing they had in common was a mutual enemy. Then there was an alliance with the French Empire. Make no mistake, the French Empire was every bit as reactionary as the British Empire. No doubt the French planned to assist the American colonials in driving out the British, and then take over the American colonies. It was the French Revolution which "threw a monkey wrench" into that plan.

Such alliances may seem strange, but are quite common, especially in times of revolution. Under such circumstances, it is frequently necessary to enter into a temporary alliance with people who are as unreliable as they are reactionary. Political necessity gives birth to "strange bedfellows". Of course, after the immediate goal is reached, the alliance is terminated.

After the American colonies won their independence, there was no longer any reason for an alliance between the northern capitalists and the southern slave owners. On the contrary, the two classes are traditional enemies. That became quite clear after the end of the Revolutionary War.

The newly minted capitalists of the north were anxious to invest their capital in the south, to build mills and factories, railroads and shipping companies. The southern "gentlemen", slave owners, were equally anxious to "maintain the status quo", to keep everything precisely the way it was. They wanted only to keep farming, using slave labour, raising their cotton and tobacco. They wanted no part of industrial development. Such an attitude is typical of all reactionaries, and is nothing short of a recipe for disaster.

By contrast, the northern capitalists had, at that time, certain progressive features, as is characteristic of capitalism in its early, pre monopoly stage. Those capitalists were determined to destroy the slave owners, as it was the slave owners who were standing in the way of "progress", which is to say, industrial development. Quite reasonably, they were of the opinion that the simplest way to destroy the slave owners was to separate them from their slaves. Impeccable logic.

The slave owners were also of that opinion, and of course they took a "dim view" of that approach, to put it mildly. In fact, they had a deep, passionate hatred for "abolitionists". Who can blame them? Over a period of many years tensions built up until they came to a head in 1861, the year of the start of the Civil War.

To this day, the American history books maintain that the Civil War took place because the states do not have the right to separate from the Union. This is consistent with their propaganda, which refuses to acknowledge the existence of classes. It is also a bare faced lie.

In fact, several decades earlier, in 1812, the country first fell apart. The six northern states, referred to as New England, declared independence. The United States did not go to war with the break away republic of New England, so that proves that the individual states have the right to separate from the Union. It was only in 1815, after the end of the British – American war, that the New England states rejoined the Union.

The American Civil War can properly be considered as a continuation of the colonial rebellion of the previous century, the Revolutionary War of 1776. At the end of the war, in 1865, the class of capitalists, the bourgeois, fully established themselves as the undisputed rulers of the country.

## CHAPTER 2

# THE SECOND AMERICAN REVOLUTION

Now in the twenty first century, the capitalists are facing crises, in the form of the virus, severe debt, massive unemployment and a president who refuses to "play by the rules". On the one hand, the bourgeoisie are more wealthy than ever. On the other hand, the working class is ever more impoverished, so that the food banks are overwhelmed. The middle class is being wiped out, so that countless workers are now unemployed. Winter is coming on, and tens of millions of working people are facing eviction, as they cannot pay the rent. The national debt is huge, and is expected to "sky rocket" in the coming months. The virus is raging out of control, and the only way to limit the spread is to close down businesses. The medical system is about to be overwhelmed, as the anticipated "surge", due to the holiday season, is expected to combine with the anticipated flu epidemic. To top it all off, the "icing on the cake", so to speak, one of their own, President Donald Trump, is being ornery. He is planning to destroy the two party system, the very system which has served the capitalists so well, since the days of the Civil War. The capitalists, the bourgeoisie, certainly have their hands full!

As if that is not bad enough, to "add insult to injury", the working class is in motion, demanding change. In particular, Black Lives Matter is demanding an end to violent police repression. In the city of Seattle, protesters have taken over a whole section of the city and managed it in a "communal" manner. This is to say that a "committee" was established, as a form of government, similar to a "Soviet" in Russia, at the time of the Russian revolution. That is not a coincidence.

There are other similarities between present day America and Russia in 1917, at the time of the revolution. At that time, in Russia, the working people were seasoned veterans. They had been schooled in the class struggle. They had "cut their teeth" in the previous revolution of 1905, at a time when the Russian Empire had been shaken to the core, but not toppled. Any and all illusions that the working people of Russia may have had, were completely smashed as the Russian government violently crushed any discontent. The Czar was exposed as the butcher that he was, concerned only with himself and his immediate family. The capitalists were no better, content to take part in the crushing of the working people. This is to say that the revolt of the workers and peasants, while not successful, provided them with a valuable "education".

After the revolution of 1905 died down, around the middle of 1907, reaction set in, as it always does. All of the Marxist leaders of the working people were thrown into prison and either killed or exiled. The Russian officials were of the opinion that it was the Marxists, also known at that time as Social Democrats or Bolsheviks, who were responsible for the revolution. So they quite reasonably assumed that with their leaders out of the picture, peace and tranquility would reign. The Czar could live as the medieval despot that he was, and the capitalists could enjoy their life of luxury, at the expense of the working people, of course. The trouble was that they could not possibly have been more mistaken. In fact, it is the people who make history, not leaders, regardless of how intelligent those leaders are.

To this day, the ruling classes of all countries, which is to say the capitalists and the nobility, cling to the belief that intelligent people, with great ideas, make history. Any and all evidence to the contrary is quietly ignored. The experience of the French revolution, in which the common people rose up and overthrew the nobility, is conveniently overlooked. They refuse to face these facts as such facts are inconvenient, and they prefer to believe that which they want to believe.

As a consequence of this, in Russia, after the 1905 revolution died down, the ruling classes, the nobility and capitalists, enjoyed a few years of blissful ignorance. They were completely unprepared for the revolutionary storm which washed over the country in 1917. In the early part of that year, February – March, the Czar was forced off the throne. It bears repeating that the "spring" revolution happened without any revolutionary leaders. The people of Russia rose up spontaneously and deposed the Czar. This is merely one example of people making history.

The abdication of Czar Nicholas did not "break the hearts" of the capitalists. With the Czar out of the way, Russia was no longer a monarchy but a republic, as a republic is a country which does not recognize a monarch. Further, according to Lenin, the democratic republic is the "best possible political shell for capitalism". He added that such a democratic republic is "curtailed, wretched, false", with the democratic rights of the people as "truncated, twisted, distorted".

The Russian democratic republic, which was established by the capitalists, immediately after the abdication of Czar Nicholas, is referred to as the Kerensky regime. It was no exception. The capitalists promised an end to the war with Germany and the Central Powers, land to the peasant who tilled that land, and the formation of a Constituent Assembly. *Except* that all this would take time…In other words, the capitalists lied, and the suffering of the common people continued.

Yet the Czar had been deposed, and that was a step in the right direction. As the Czar was out of the way, Lenin was able to return to Russia, in April of 1917. The working people were very happy to see him, their leader, while the secret police were less than thrilled. In fact, they saw Lenin as the biggest threat to the rule of the capitalists, as indeed he was. Accordingly, they set out to kill Lenin.

With that in mind, Lenin went into hiding and prepared for the upcoming revolution. Over the course of the summer, he wrote that which is considered to be his greatest masterpiece, the article State And Revolution. In that article, Lenin outlined the tasks of the working people when seizing political power. In particular, he stressed the importance of smashing the existing state machinery, that which has been set up to crush the working class, and replacing it with a new, proletarian state apparatus, in order to crush the capitalists. This new state apparatus is referred to as the Dictatorship Of the Proletariat. It is only in this way that the working people, the proletariat, can maintain state power, after the revolution.

As the current situation in North America is so similar to the situation of Russia, 1917, that article should be read by all people taking part in the current American revolution. Many of the people taking part in the uprising are veterans, those who took part in the occupy movement as well as the anti war movement of the sixties. Those are the "old salts" who have been tempered in the struggle, and they, in turn, will help to train the "raw recruits".

Recently, three separate republics have taken shape in America, on the east coast, the west coast, and the midwest. Any day now, they could declare independence. For that matter, the colonies of Hawaii, Alaska and Puerto Rico could go their own way. It is just a matter of time, probably a short time. We had best be prepared. Otherwise, the American empire could break up to form separate capitalist republics. This is referred to as going "from the frying pan, into the fire".

This is another way of saying that working people need proper leaders, Marxist leaders, Communist leaders, those who call for the Dictatorship Of the Proletariat. Those who claim to be Marxist or Communist but deny the necessity of the Dictatorship Of the Proletariat, are social chauvinists. They are in the service of the capitalists, and they are the enemy.

Bear in mind the words of Engels: *Without a revolutionary theory, there can be no revolutionary motion!* At a time of revolutionary upheaval, such as we are now experiencing, this must be stressed. It is up to conscious people, Marxists, to bring to the working class the awareness of themselves as a class, with their own class interests.

With that in mind, allow me to point out the obvious. Numerous middle class people have recently joined the ranks of the proletariat, if only because they have been ruined by capitalism. The remainder of the middle class will soon follow suit. The bourgeoisie will see to that! Such people, freshly minted proletarians, are class conscious, aware of the revolutionary theories of Marx and Lenin. Feel free to share that knowledge with your class comrades. Raise the level of awareness of the working class. Prepare for the Dictatorship Of the Proletariat. Take part in the formation of a true Communist Party, DOP, in that DOP stands for the Dictatorship Of the Proletariat. Such a Communist Party is desperately needed.

No doubt many people will complain that I am not being fair, that I am placing a heavy burden on a relatively few people. To such people I can only respond that you are right. It is not fair. Life is not fair. It is what it is.

Now is the time to form the American Communist Party, DOP.

## CHAPTER 3

# DONALD TRUMP AND THE DISUNITED STATES OF AMERICA

The recent presidential election in the United States brought to the surface some deep divisions within the country. All across the country, people are protesting, marching in cities and towns. Even students are joining in, as classrooms are being emptied.

The situation changed dramatically in one day as Trump went from a political laughing stock to the president – elect. The polling companies were just as mistaken concerning the federal election as they were concerning the Brexit, the British exit from the European Union. The self styled political experts were caught flat footed as they were all convinced that Hillary Clinton was sure to win the election. Now these same "experts" are scrambling to explain that which they cannot understand.

The fact is that the revolutionary movement has now spread around the world and is currently raging in North America. Countless people, those who were formerly apathetic. are now "waking up", as they put it, taking an interest in their lives. They previously referred to themselves as the 99 percent, while referring to the "super rich", the billionaires, as the 1 percent. The fact that those terms are no longer in use is an encouraging sign. It indicates an increased level of awareness on their part. Of course, the working class is technically referred to as the proletariat, while the monopoly capitalist class, the billionaires, are referred to as the bourgeoisie. It is the middle class, the small business owners, who are referred to as the petty bourgeois. I mention this for the benefit of the members of the working class who are just now becoming politically aware. Welcome!

The political pundits either do not or cannot understand that this is class struggle, the working class against the capitalist class. The members of the working class who are taking part in this revolution are also largely unaware, rising up spontaneously, not conscious of the fact that they are part of a world wide revolution, one that is destined to overthrow the rule of the capitalists.

Here in North America, the class struggle has the bright shining virtue of simplicity, in that other classes, such as the peasantry and the middle class, have been largely wiped out. For this, we can thank the capitalists, the billionaires. They are doing a fine job of digging their own graves!

This is the age of monopoly capitalism, technically referred to as imperialism, which is the highest stage of capitalism. Before capitalism reached this stage of monopoly, there was competition between the capitalists, so that there were a great many small mills and factories across the country. These helped to support various small towns. These businesses provided productive, reasonably well paying jobs, so that the people who worked there usually owned their own house, had a car or two in the garage, and were able to take a family vacation once a year. As they were generally able to make ends meet on one paycheck, those days are now rather nostalgically referred to as the "good old days".

In fact, those days were not all that good at all, but compared to the situation in which we now find ourselves, those days were downright golden!

In those days of competitive capitalism, the people who owned those small mills and factories were referred to as small business owners. They referred to themselves as business men or entrepreneurs, members of the middle class, technically referred to as the petty bourgeois. For the most part, they invested their limited capital in factories which produced such items as shoes, clothing, lumber and such. The products were then sold locally or more frequently shipped abroad, which is referred to as the export of goods. This export of goods is characteristic of capitalism in its early, competitive stage.

The situation was such that the workers were enjoying a reasonably comfortable lifestyle, grateful to the business owner who was providing them with a productive job. The workers in turn took pride in their work, and went out of their way to "go the extra mile" for the company. "An honest days work for an honest days pay" was the slogan. The workers were proud of the company for which they worked, and were also proud of the product they produced. In those days, the workers were loyal to the company for which they worked.

This sentiment of loyalty, on the part of the workers, was not reciprocated. The owner of the business was focused on making a profit, and not just any profit, but the maximum possible profit. So on the one hand it was a matter of forcing the workers to work as hard as possible, while paying them as little as possible, while on the other hand it was a matter of putting the competition out of business. Never mind that in the process of putting the competition out of business, he was also putting other workers out of a job. Such details were of no concern to the small time capitalist of yesteryear, just as they are of no concern to the modern day monopoly capitalist.

Yet, nature took its course, so to speak, and one after another, most small businesses either went broke or were bought out by the big businesses, until nothing was left but the monopolies.

It may be objected that there is still the odd small business in existence, producing some goods, usually specialty items, just as there is, to this day, the odd locally owned corner store. To this, I can only respond that we still have the occasional old style type writer in existence, complete with the mule headed old fool who is pecking at it with one finger. One is about as common place as the other. Both are going the way of the dodo bird.

This in no way changes the fact that these small businesses, which are characteristic of capitalism in its pre monopoly stage, are a thing of the past. The people who owned those small businesses, the middle class, have been swallowed up by the monopolies and are now history.

By contrast, we now live in the age of monopoly capitalism, or imperialism, which is characterized by the export of capital, as opposed to the export of goods.

With that in mind, consider the fact that Trump is a billionaire, a member of the monopoly class of capitalists we refer to as the bourgeoisie. As president, he dramatically reduced the taxes on the banks and corporations, in the interest of "creating more jobs". He also placed a tariff on goods coming into the country. Of course, this resulted in massive lay offs, as jobs were eliminated.

This calls for a little explanation. Such a massive tax cut on the banks and corporations had the effect of providing the corporations with a huge "infusion of capital". This gave the capitalists a number of options. They could embark on a massive upgrade of factories, which means increased mechanization in order to increase production while laying off workers, or possibly shutting down existing factories, with the idea of relocating them to a different country, or simply shutting down factories in order to reduce the supply of goods within the country, while raising prices on the limited supply, thus increasing profit. Of course, a combination of those options is also possible.

The tariffs on goods coming into the country helps to allow the capitalists to raise prices on goods produced in the country. This in no way discourages the capitalists from sending their factories to a different country. Still less does it discourage the capitalists from closing factories within the country, in order to create a shortage.

As for those who think that this is a rather cynical attitude, I can only point out that the capitalists are concerned only with making a profit. After all, that is the one and only reason they are in business. They do not care in the slightest for working people. Besides, if I was a billionaire and a corporate executive and found myself in that position, those are precisely the options I would consider.

The point must be driven home to the working class, and especially to the people who are taking part in this revolution, that Trump is not exceptional. On the contrary, he is merely a typical capitalist. He is worth many billions, yet pays no taxes. In fact, he has not paid any taxes in many years. This is a fact of which he is most proud. All capitalist feel that way. The less taxes they pay, the better.

This is the age of imperialism, monopoly capitalism, and as such, we can expect "reaction, right down the line", according to Lenin. He explained this supremely well in his article, Imperialism, the Highest Stage of Capitalism. It is an article I highly recommend.

Under capitalism, and especially monopoly capitalism, the politicians who are elected to office are careful to pass laws that protect the billionaires, the monopoly capitalists. These elected officials are no more than flunkies of the bourgeoisie, usually mere millionaires, at best. The exception is Trump, a billionaire who decided to run for president, on impulse. No one was more surprised than Trump to find that he had won the election.

For the most part, those who are loyal servants of the capitalists tend to be thrown a few scraps, much as we throw a bone to a dog. As an example, the former first lady has served the capitalists for many years, and as a bonus, was recently paid several hundred thousand dollars to "give a speech". Her reward for years of faithful service. We can expect such rewards to become less frequent, as the crises in capitalism intensify.

Those who have sold themselves to the capitalists, including the leaders of the working class, can expect the "gravy train" to cease. These "labour lieutenants of the capitalist class" will then have no choice but to reenter the working class, and they must be welcomed back, but not trusted. Those who turn their coats once, can be expected to do so again.

No doubt there are readers who do not know a reactionary from a recliner. So with that in mind, I will mention that a reactionary is not an expensive sofa but an individual who is stuck in the old ways, absolutely opposes change, and wants everything to stay exactly the way it is. As society is in a constant state of change, especially now with advances in technology proceeding at a breakneck pace, such a state of mind is a recipe for disaster.

It is also a fact that Trump is a first class demagogue. For those readers who may think that a demagogue is a breed of dog, I can only respond that it is not, but you are close. In fact, a demagogue is a political leader who makes use of popular prejudices and makes false claims in order to gain power. Hitler was perhaps one of the finest demagogues of modern times, but he is facing fierce competition in the form of President Trump. That man is a first class liar, but then he has been honing those lying skills all his life. Now that he has taken up tweeting, we can no longer say that he only lies when his lips are moving. He also lies when he tweets!

To return to the working people who are protesting, the immediate problem is to raise their level of awareness. They have got to be made aware that it is a class struggle, the working class against the capitalists. Trump is merely the most obvious symbol. To replace him with some other servant of the capitalists, would serve no purpose. The capitalists must be overthrown, and this can be accomplished only through revolution. That class of parasites, the bourgeoisie, must be destroyed, absolutely crushed.

The whole political system must be overthrown. The existing state apparatus, which has been set up to exploit and oppress the working class, has to be destroyed. In its place, a new state apparatus will have to be established, a working class state apparatus, run by and for the working class, with the one goal of crushing the desperate and determined resistance of the capitalists. This state apparatus is referred to as the Dictatorship Of the Proletariat.

It will be absolutely necessary to set up this proletarian state apparatus, as after the revolution, the resistance of the billionaires will be increased ten fold. They will spare no effort, will resort to any subterfuge, any lie, any deceit, to restore their "paradise lost".

After the successful socialist revolution, all businesses will be in the hands of the working class, the class that has state power. The mills, factories, mines, railroads, banks, shipping lines, communications companies and internet, will be run by and for the working class. They will be run for the benefit of all working people, *not* for a profit, *not* for the chosen few.

As anyone who has ever worked in a factory can testify, the workers can run the factories far more efficiently than the capitalists. That is true of all businesses. For that reason, after the revolution, the standard of living of the working class, the proletariat, will rise dramatically.

At the same time, the standard of living of the capitalists, those who previously lived in the "lap of luxury", will fall dramatically. Not that they will be living in poverty, as we can provide them with useful, productive work. Perhaps building railroad tracks is a job they can handle. After the revolution, we want everyone to be engaged in useful work.

For now, the main thing is to prepare for the Dictatorship Of the Proletariat. The level of awareness of the working class, or at least the most advanced stratum of the workers, must be raised to the level of Marxists. These advanced workers will in turn lead the less advanced.

The best way to accomplish this, if not the only way, is through a proper American Communist Party, DOP, in that DOP stands for Dictatorship Of the Proletariat. The lack of a proper Communist Party is a serious matter. It is to be hoped that the recent additions to the working class, the former middle class intellectuals, will rise to the occasion and create such a Party.

We will know that we are on the right track when the banners and signs read:

# DOWN WITH CAPITALISM!

# SCIENTIFIC SOCIALISM!

# DICTATORSHIP OF THE PROLETARIAT!

# WORKERS OF THE WORLD, UNITE!

## CHAPTER 4

# LIFE WITH TRUMP AS PRESIDENT

As I write this, Trump has been president for almost four years. Immediately after his inauguration, millions of Americans, mainly women, took to the streets in protest. As well, around the world, countless others marched in solidarity with their American comrades. These protests were largely disciplined and peaceful, aside from the criminal elements who took advantage of the situation to commit acts of looting and vandalism.

There can be no question that the American revolutionary motion now places the American workers in the vanguard of the world revolutionary movement. Very recently, there has been a slight lull in the movement. This is not to say that the revolution is dying down. During major battles, there are occasional pauses, in which the commanders prepare a fresh offensive. The next major offensive of the working class could be decisive.

Without doubt, the current situation is revolutionary. The Corona Virus pandemic is raging out of control. It is being compared to the flu epidemic of 1918. The medical system is close to being overwhelmed, with hospitals filled to capacity. A further anticipated "surge", combined with the flu season, is expected to send the fatality rate much higher. The unemployment rate is at levels not seen since the Great Depression. Winter is approaching, and it is anticipated that further tens of millions of people will soon be homeless, evicted because they cannot pay the rent. The food banks cannot keep up with demand, as so many people are hungry. The national debt is at a level formerly thought to be inconceivable, and is expected to rise much higher.

On the other hand, from the bourgeois perspective, the situation is rosy. The stock market continues to climb, to reach record highs. It is soaring. The billionaires, the bourgeoisie, are becoming ever more wealthy. Who says an economic Depression is bad for business? There is a reason President Trump, himself a billionaire, is playing golf. Life is good.

In the face of all this calamity, the mainstream press is focused on the federal election. They refer to Biden as the "President Elect", which he is not. Nor is he the "Messiah", although the way the journalists behave, you would think he was. The journalists would also have us believe that Trump already has "one foot in prison". Possibly it never occurred to those optimistic souls that there is a reason he is playing golf. Possibly there is a reason Trump appears to be unconcerned.

Possibly he is not concerned. Possibly he knows something we do not. Possibly that something has to do with the Twelfth Amendment.

The Twelfth Amendment to the Constitution make it quite clear that the Electors determine the president and the vice president. The men who wrote that Amendment, the Founding Fathers of the country, were concerned that the common people, the "rag tag and bob tail", would want a voice in the governing of the country. God forbid! That is the reason for the Twelfth.

The Electors, the Chosen Ones, will vote on December 14, and the vote will be counted on January 6. At that time we will know the president to be sworn in on January 20. Or not, if no one receives a majority of the votes. Perhaps someone should advise the journalists of this!

It is entirely possible that the Electors will choose Trump. The reason for this is that the lawyers who are working for Trump have been busy, advising the state legislatures that they have every legal right to appoint Electors who will vote for him. Those lawyers have been busy, working "behind the scenes", earning their pay.

In particular, the "personal lawyer" for Trump has been doing a fine job of documenting voter fraud. He has "spelled out", in great detail, the manner in which the elections are "rigged". The man certainly knows what he is talking about! No doubt he speaks from experience. It is very likely he has been rigging elections all his life!

It is entirely possible that the results of that election will set off a "fire storm" of revolutionary movement. The country is a "powder keg", so that any spark could cause an explosion. Of course we have no way of knowing the precise spark, before it happens.

On the other hand, we do know what to expect. It was the expert on revolution, Lenin, who explained it well in his article, Left Wing Communism, An Infantile Disorder. It was written in 1921, several years after the successful Russian Revolution. As it is of such vital importance, I have chosen to quote it in full:

> "The fundamental law of revolution, confirmed by all revolutions, and particularly by all three Russian revolutions of the twentieth century, is as follows: it is not sufficient for the revolution that the exploited and oppressed masses understand the impossibility of living in the old way and demand change; for the revolution it is necessary that the exploiters should not be able to live and rule as of old. Only when the masses do not want the old regime, and when the rulers are unable to govern as of old, then only can the revolution succeed. This truth may be expressed in other words: revolution is impossible without an all national crisis, affecting both the exploiters and exploited. It follows that for the revolution it is essential first, that a majority of the workers (or at least a majority of the conscious, thinking, politically active workers) should fully understand the necessity for a revolution, and be ready to sacrifice their lives for it; second, that the ruling class

be in a state of governmental crisis which attracts even the most backward masses into politics. It is a sign of every real revolution, this rapid ten fold or even hundred fold increase in the number of representatives of the toiling and oppressed masses, heretofore apathetic, who are able to carry on a political fight which weakens the government and facilitates its overthrow by the revolutionaries."

I maintain that the "fundamental law of revolution" is being met, at least here in North America, and very likely in other countries of the world. It is clear that the "exploited and oppressed" are finding it impossible to live in the old way and are demanding change. It is also clear that the "exploiters", which is to say the billionaires, the bourgeoisie, can no longer rule in the old way.

Trump is determined to remain in office, and his lawyers have advised him that the best way to do this, is by *abiding by the law!* That is rather ironic, as Trump has made a career of breaking every law which he finds to be inconvenient. It just so happens that there is one law which he finds to be convenient, and that law is the Twelfth Amendment to the Constitution. Rather than break that law, he plans to use it. The leaders of the two mainstream political parties, Democrats and Republicans, are the people who have been breaking that law!

Since the days of the Civil War, the two party system has served the capitalists well. The leaders of each party determine a candidate to run for president, and that candidate then chooses a "running mate", a candidate for vice president. Then comes the formality of a general election -which is easily rigged- as well as the formality of the "Elector Vote" -which is even more easily rigged- followed by the ceremonial "swearing in" as president. All of which is in direct violation of the Twelfth Amendment!

For the last several months, the lawyers who work for Trump have been advising the state legislatures, as well as those who are appointed as Electors, that they can "vote their conscience" -as if they have any conscience!- or at least vote for anyone but Biden. Assuming that happens -and there is a good chance of this- then the matter will likely end up before the Supreme Court. We can also expect the Supreme Court to strike down any and all state laws which interfere in a federal election, effectively destroying the two party system.

This is another way of saying that the "exploiters", in this case the capitalists, will "not be able to live and rule as of old". That satisfies part of the "fundamental law of revolution". The other aspect of that law -perhaps the flip side of the coin?- "the exploited and oppressed masses understand the impossibility of living in the old way and demand change", is also being met.

This is *not* to imply that the revolution is about to run its own course, that the capitalists will be overthrown, and we will then enter an "age of Aquarius", a time of peace and tranquility. That is not about to happen. People still need leaders, and that is where conscious people come in, those who are aware of the revolutionary theories of Marx and Lenin. Fortunately, the capitalists have graciously sent, to the working class, numerous such people. Mind you, not all of the people sent, by the capitalists, are terribly happy about this. In fact, some of them are downright bitter. They are not at all thrilled by the fact that they have been forced to lower their standard of living. Their hopes and dreams of living out their years in relative comfort, in a quiet middle class neighbourhood, have been shattered. For that matter, visions of joining the ranks of the billionaires have been ground into the dust. They have received their "reward" for years of faithful service. The best years of their life have been devoted to the cause of contributing to the "bottom line" of the company. In return, they have been discarded, thrown out like an old newspaper. Yet the question that comes to mind is: What did they expect?

Such people should be well aware that it is standard business practice to increase production through mechanization. In that way, as a bonus, workers are laid off. As a result of this, less supervisory personnel are required. At some point, it is decided that certain supervisors have to go. Or, then again, the capitalists may lay someone off, *because they can!*

To such people, I can only say, buck up! If you give it some thought, you well see that the future is bright. Still doubtful? Bear with me. You will see that I am right.

Face the fact that you have "climbed the ladder of success" as high as you could go, under capitalism. You could go no further, for whatever reason. As that is the case, the only way you can rise to a higher level is by *first falling!* Now you have fallen into the ranks of the proletariat, and you have the opportunity to rise to great heights, under the socialist system!

No doubt you are a conscious person, aware of the revolutionary theories of Marx and Lenin. Under capitalism, as a middle class person, you had to hide that knowledge. There is no longer any need to be "shy". The capitalists are no longer capable of threatening you with career suicide, as you *no longer have a career!* You can now share that knowledge with your brethren, your comrades, your fellow proletarians, as you have nothing to lose, and everything to gain.

Feel free to raise the level of awareness of the working class. They have come "a ways", as they no longer refer to themselves as the "99 percent", just as they no longer refer to the monopoly capitalists as the "1 percent". Yet this is still consciousness in an "embryonic form", as Lenin phrased it. Without assistance from an outside source, it can go no further.

Lenin explained this quite clearly in his article, What Is To Be Done? Allow me to quote from that article: "The history of all countries shows that the working class, exclusively by its own effort, is able to develop only trade union consciousness... The theory of socialism, however, grew out of the philosophic, historical and economic theories that were elaborated by the educated representatives of the propertied classes, the intellectuals. According to their social status, the founders of modern scientific socialism, Marx and Engels, themselves belonged to the bourgeois intelligentsia."

As you can see, there is a place for you in the revolutionary movement. People need leaders, and that is where you come in. There is a desperate need for a proper Communist Party to provide the leadership. Bear in mind that in Czarist Russia, 1895, such a Party was formed, under far more difficult circumstances, by a few young, middle class intellectuals. One of those intellectuals was Vladimir Ilyich Ulyanov, otherwise known as Lenin.

As they managed to form a Party under such circumstances, no doubt the formation of an American Communist Party is also possible. In fact, it should be much easier, as modern technology provides us with various tools. We would be fools not to use those tools, such as the internet, computers and various programs. There is no need to gather in one location, and there must be ways to block the government spooks.

After the revolution, under socialism, we will still need specialists, and that includes engineers and administrators. Such key personnel will be placed in positions of authority, and paid accordingly, far more than the average workers. They will also be allowed to promote to higher positions, something which is denied to most professionals, under capitalism.

Rest assured, your past will not be held against you. Further, it may help to think of the years you spent in the service of the capitalists as an education, because that is precisely what it was. Now focus that drive and determination on preparing for the Dictatorship Of the Proletariat.

# CHAPTER 5

# SOCIALISM AND DEMOCRACY

The revolutionary motion which is currently raging across America is not an isolated incident. Similar uprisings are happening in various countries around the world. It is doubtful that this is a coincidence. Previous revolutions have been confined to one country, or at best, several countries in one part of the world. Such examples include Russia in 1905 and 1917, Cuba in 1959, Iran in 1979, Germany in 1848, and France in 1789. Clearly, something has changed, and changed quite dramatically.

It is very likely, that certain "something", which has changed, is capitalism. It has reached the stage of monopoly capitalism, technically referred to as imperialism. It has spread around the world, sinking its hooks ever deeper into the economies of the world, tying together those economies. It is quite possible that it has also tied together the revolutionary motion of the world.

Without doubt, modern communications have made it possible to broadcast immediately around the world, making it far more difficult for the capitalists to deceive the people.

Be that as it may, the fact is that the revolutionary motion in America is exceptionally deep and strong. By contrast, in the nineteen sixties, there were various popular movements, which included the anti war movement, the women's movement, the black movement and the American Indian movement. As they grew in strength, they came ever closer together. At the peak of the movement, every university in the country went on strike, in protest against the war in Viet Nam, and half a million people marched on Washington.

Compare this to the revolutionary motion that is now sweeping the country. It is far stronger than the motion of the sixties, even at its peak. The movement of the black people, in the form of Black Lives Matter, has merged with the working class movement, and the movement as a whole is being led by women. Further, the marches are largely peaceful, well disciplined. The same cannot be said of the marches of the sixties, many of which were marred by acts of vandalism and looting. True, there is the occasional act of looting in the marches of today, but they are exceptional. The women of today have every reason to be proud of themselves. For perhaps the first time in history, a revolution is being led by women!

The mainstream press is following this revolutionary motion quite closely, without understanding it. The journalists are quite accurately reporting events as they are happening, even though they are confused. For that reason, they are asking people why they are protesting. Many people respond that they are marching for their children, as they want their children to have a better life. This is very true, just as it is also true that most people do not know the reason they are marching. As yet, they are not aware that they are taking part in a revolution. In fact, during a revolution, people rise up spontaneously, not conscious of the fact that they are members of a working class, and that they are rising up against a class of capitalists. Still less are they aware of the fact that they are part of a world wide socialist revolutionary movement. But then the working class in not aware of itself as a class.

This is certainly not acceptable. The awareness of the working class, which is called "class consciousness", must be brought to the people taking part in this revolution, and it can only come from an outside source. That outside source is middle class intellectuals.

The fact is that we live in a class society, and further, the monopoly capitalists, the billionaires, form a class of people who are scientifically referred to as the bourgeoisie. They stand in sharp contrast to the vast majority of working people, those who are scientifically referred to as the proletariat. Whereas the billionaires have more money than they can possibly spend, the proletarians have nothing to sell but their labor power. Here in North America, the other classes, such as the peasantry and the middle class, the petty bourgeois, have been all but wiped out. If nothing else, this simplifies the class struggle.

It is the billionaires, the bourgeoisie, which is the class of people who are in charge. They rule. The country is referred to as a democratic republic, which is the best possible political shell for capitalism. For that reason, every few years, the workers get to decide which particular members of the ruling class are sent to the various capitals, in order to misrepresent them. This in no way changes the fact that the bourgeoisie are in charge. We live under their rule, the dictatorship of the bourgeoisie.

True, the working class has some limited democratic rights -truncated, twisted, distorted democratic rights- under their rule, the rule of the bourgeoisie. This is certainly not acceptable, and must change. The working class must seize power and establish socialism, and this can only happen through revolution. At that time, the state apparatus which has been set up by the capitalists, in order to crush the working class, must be destroyed. At that time, a new state apparatus must be established, in order to crush the desperate and determined resistance of the bourgeoisie, as they try to restore their "paradise lost". That new state apparatus is referred to as the Dictatorship Of the Proletariat.

It should be noted that in both Russia and China, socialism was established after violent revolution. But then the capitalists were able to return to power, as they were not completely crushed, or at least not with sufficient enthusiasm. After the forthcoming American revolution, we must be sure to not repeat that mistake.

As for those who maintain that a dictatorship is not at all democratic, may I refer you to the "birthplace of democracy", which is the city state of Athens, in Greece. The school books say that it was the first truly democratic form of government, in that the citizens got together and voted, and it was majority rule. There is some truth to this, as far as it goes. It does not go very far.

The school books do not say that only the property owners were allowed to vote. As only men were allowed to own property in Athens, that immediately excluded half the population. Then too, there were a great many slaves in Athens, for more slaves than free people, but of course they too were excluded. It is also a fact that most free Athenians were too poor to own property, so they too were excluded. Then there were the immigrants, but regardless of how much property they owned, they too were excluded.

With that in mind, it is safe to say that for every voter in Athens, there were possibly one hundred Athenians who could not vote. The birthplace of democracy was truly a case of the "1 percent" ruling over the "99 percent".

In short, democracy in Athens was a form of class rule. The class of people who owned property ruled over the various classes of people who did not own property, and that included the women, slaves, tradesmen, immigrants and peasants. To this day, democracy is still a form of class rule. The only thing that has changed is the fact that new classes have come into existence.

In particular, the industrial revolution has given rise to two new classes of people, the capitalists and the workers. The capitalists, or bourgeois, are those who own the mills, mines, factories, railroads, shipping lines, communications companies, internet and anything of any considerable value. Their "antipode", or the class opposite them, the working class or proletariat, was created at the same time. Of course we work for the bourgeois, in that we sell them our labor power.

Whereas in Athens it was the property owners who ruled, now in America it is the bourgeoisie who rule. The classes have changed, but the fact of class rule has not changed. It is also a fact that in Athens, the slaves knew they were members of a class. By contrast, under capitalism, the working class is not aware of itself as a class. The conditions of life, of the proletariat, do not lead to that awareness.

This in no way changes the fact that there are times when the working class spontaneously gets into motion. This is one of those times. Workers are now gravitating towards socialism, sensing that it is not just a matter of fighting Trump, but also a matter of fighting the whole system that he represents, which is to say capitalism. This is still not class consciousness, but an important step in the right direction. The poster of one of the protesters made this quite clear, in that it stated:

# WOMEN OF THE WORLD, UNITE!

That is close to class consciousness, as it is very similar to a Marxist slogan. Yet it contains no class content. It also conveniently overlooks the fact that there are women of the world who are billionaires, members of the class of people whom we refer to as the bourgeoisie. Such women are not about to join any women's group, at least not one which is marching for revolutionary reasons. The only reason such a woman could have for joining such a group, would be to divert it onto some harmless path of social reform. Capitalism is based on class, not gender. Female billionaires are every bit as reactionary as their male counterparts. They merely tend to be a bit more devious.

In particular, the Trump family contains several such individuals. It is supremely unlikely that any of those women are about to take part in the revolution. It is not in their interest to do so. They have a great deal to lose, such as mountains of money. Then there is the not so little matter of their freedom, which they also cherish. Perhaps someone should draw this to the attention of the women who are taking part in the revolution.

To return to the subject of democracy, no doubt soon the capitalists will be saying that a dictatorship is not democratic. In fact, a democracy is a *method of rule*, a means by which one class crushes another class. In ancient Greece, it was the class of landowners who ruled, and crushed all other classes. In ancient Rome, it was the slave owners who ruled, and crushed the slaves. At other times in history, the nobility have ruled. In all cases, one class rules. The *method of rule* may change, and democracy is one such method of rule.

As soon as the revolutionary motion becomes class conscious, then the posters and banners will call for the Dictatorship Of the Proletariat. At that time, the capitalists and their loyal servants will complain that such a Dictatorship is not "pure democracy". In this they are absolutely correct, as there is no such thing as "pure democracy".

It is up to Marxists to make working people aware that there is something referred to as an "oxymoron", which is a "contradiction in terms". Several popular examples of this should help to educate the members of the public. Most people are familiar with the term "friendly fire". We can point out that bullets are not friendly, nor are they unfriendly. They just are.

Then there is the term "secret bombing". Of course, it is not possible to drop bombs on people and keep it a secret. People who are being bombed tend not to keep it a secret. In fact, they talk about it constantly. The most ridiculous example is that of "holy war". War is a great many things, but "holy" in not one of them. When put in these terms, people can understand them.

This brings us to our original oxymoron, "pure democracy". As "democracy" is nothing other than a method of rule, it *cannot be pure!* It is a means by which one class crushes another class. Under capitalism, a democratic republic is one in which the capitalists, the bourgeoisie, rule over the working class, the proletariat. It is a democracy for the bourgeois, but a dictatorship for the working class. The dictatorship of the bourgeoisie.

By contrast, the Dictatorship Of the Proletariat is also a method of class rule, except that the vast majority, the working class, the proletariat, crushes the tiny minority of capitalists, the bourgeoisie. For the proletariat, it is a democracy, but for the bourgeoisie, it is a dictatorship.

It is absolutely necessary to exercise dictatorship over the capitalists, to crush them, as they are the same people who are responsible for the butchery in Viet Nam, as well as the slaughter of nine eleven. They are not the sort of people who respond to "sweet reason". Nor are they about to resign themselves to a life of manual labor. As after the revolution, we want everyone to be useful, and they have no skills, perhaps pick and shovel work is a job they can handle.

## CHAPTER 6

# UNITING THE LEFT IN AMERICA

America is one of the few places in the world which denies the existence of classes! To be more precise, the existence of classes in America is denied. The capitalists would have us believe that the Revolutionary War of 1776 established an independent republic, one which does not recognize any monarch, and at the same time abolished classes in the new republic. Nothing can be farther from the truth.

The nonsense being propagated, by the capitalists, is to the effect that under a democratic republic, all citizens are equal. Everyone has a vote, and it is majority rule. The trouble is that a great many common people, members of the public, working people, tend to agree with this. (I should note that such people also tend to frown upon being referred to as "masses", so I try to avoid that term. It sounds rather impersonal.) That in no way changes the fact that the belief is wide spread, so that it deserves our attention.

We can point out to people that we live in a class society. Our membership in a class is determined by our "relationship to the means of production". This is another scientific term with which working people must become familiar. At least, the most advanced members of the working class must learn these terms. They in turn can explain it to the less advanced.

Those who own the "means of production", which is to say the factories, mills, mines and so forth, as well as the railroads, shipping lines, communications companies, internet and in fact anything of any considerable value, are referred to as capitalists. The members of this class are referred to as "bourgeois". Those who own small businesses are referred to as "petty bourgeois", or middle class, while those who own huge banks and corporations, are referred to as "bourgeoisie". The petty bourgeois tend to be mere millionaires, at best, while the bourgeoisie are billionaires, or multi billionaires. The most obvious such billionaire is Trump.

In stark contrast to the capitalists, or bourgeois, are the members of the class opposite to them, referred to as the "antipode". That class is of course the working class, or the "proletariat", and members of that class are referred to as "proletarians". Most members of that class refer to themselves as workers, because that is precisely what they are. Proletarians have no property, and are reduced to selling themselves, or their labor power, usually by the hour. For that reason, workers are referred to as "wage slaves", as that is precisely the case.

In other parts of the world, there are other classes, such as the nobility and peasantry. In fact, the remnants or other classes still exist in America. The family farmer is a peasant, but is almost completely wiped out. As well, there are still a few middle class people, those who own a small business, but they are being squeezed ever tighter by the monopolies, forced into bankruptcy. The current crises in capitalism are merely accelerating the process. If nothing else, this simplifies the class struggle.

As the conditions of life of the working class do not lead to the awareness of classes, this awareness must be brought to them from an outside source. That outside source is of course middle class intellectuals. As a great many such middle class intellectuals are currently being ruined, forced into the ranks of the proletariat, they are bringing with them their awareness of classes. Now is their "time to shine", to "rise to the occasion", to take part in the creation of a proper American Communist Party, Dictatorship Of the Proletariat. Such an organization is needed in order to lead the working class, in the upcoming revolution. As I have covered this in a previous article, there is no need to repeat it.

Only such a truly Marxist Communist Party can unite and lead the proletariat. That is a tall order, as there are currently a number of organizations in the country which claim to be socialist or Marxist or Communist. As well, there are various groups which are focused on particular reforms. Some of these outfits we can unite with, if only temporarily, while others are in the service of the capitalists. All are commonly referred to as "Leftist", while Marxists are generally referred to as "radical

Leftists". By contrast, those who serve the capitalists are referred to as "right wing". These expressions are not mine.

It was Lenin who explained that there are three trends within the revolutionary movement. There are the scientific socialists, referred to as Marxists or Communist, and then there are the utopian socialists, or centrists. As well, there are the social chauvinists, those who are socialists in works, chauvinists in deeds. There is some movement between the trends of the centre and that of the chauvinists, in that individuals of one trend occasionally drift to the other.

As Marxists, it is up to us to distinguish between the centrists and the chauvinists. We can work with the centrists, as they tend to be honest, reasonable, well intentioned people. For the most part, they are focused on one reform or another, while maintaining that socialism is a good idea. We can join them in marches and demonstrations, while carrying our own posters and banners, which call for revolution and scientific socialism, in the form of the Dictatorship Of the Proletariat.

By contrast, the social chauvinists are in the service of the capitalists. Their one and only goal, their reason for activity within the working class movement, is to divert it onto some harmless path of social reform. They are dead set opposed to revolution, and especially the Dictatorship Of the Proletariat. They will do their best to sabotage any revolutionary uprising. They are the enemy, and we want no part of them. We must make it very clear to the working people that we consider them to be the enemy, because they are.

This in no way changes the fact that we are facing a very powerful enemy, in the form of the monopoly capitalists, the bourgeoisie. Even though numerically small, they are well entrenched, with a most impressive state apparatus. We are going to need all the help we can get, in order to overthrow them. That is the reason it is so important to distinguish between our friends and our enemies. The *social chauvinists are our enemies!*

With that in mind, may I stress the importance of uniting the Left. That is difficult, but not impossible, as there are a great many groups on the Left, and a few of them truly hate each other. That is unfortunate, but an obstacle which can be overcome. We must point out to all Leftist groups that we do not have to love each other, just as we do not have to socialize. It is just a matter of coming together against a common enemy, the capitalists. After the revolution, after the overthrow of the capitalists, after we establish scientific socialism in the form of the Dictatorship Of the Proletariat, then we can hash out our differences.

Modern communications, in the form of computers and the internet, have provided us with valuable tools. We can use these tools to send emails to various groups, calling for unity, a common front against the capitalists. Not all groups have to agree to our goal of scientific socialism. As long as they do not oppose it, we can work together.

# CHAPTER 7

# DEMOCRACY AND REVOLUTIONARY ORGANIZATIONS IN AMERICA

As the crisis in capitalism continues to intensify, so too the revolutionary movement of the working class also intensifies. Countless Americans have now been roused to a frenzy, infuriated that the virus is raging out of control, unemployment is rampant, bankruptcy is widespread, evictions and homelessness are common place, the medical system is close to collapse, and the *president is playing golf!*

And why not? The stock market is reaching record highs. Profits are soaring, as the economic policies, for which Trump takes credit, have enabled the capitalists to become ever more wealthy. The billionaires club, of which Trump is a member, has now been blessed with more billions. Life is good.

At least, life is good for the handful of "super rich", the billionaires, the members of the class of people who are referred to as the bourgeoisie. For the common people, the working class, it is a "whole different ball game".

There is currently a slight "lull" in the revolutionary motion, as many people are focused on the presidential election. It is just a matter of time, and probably a very short time, before the motion flares up again. We can expect it to flare up with a vengeance!

Many members of the working class are now veterans of the class struggle. In fact, this current movement can be considered to be a continuation of the occupy movement of several years ago. That movement was crushed, with considerable brutality, and in the process, countless working people were tempered. Any illusions they may have had, concerning the idea that their democratically elected leaders were in their service, were dispelled. The elected leaders serve the capitalist class.

Now the people who took part in the occupy movement are veterans, and are coaching the younger members of the present generation of protesters. For that matter, the older ones are veterans of the anti war movement of the "sixties". Partly for that reason, the current revolutionary movement is much finer and stronger.

It is safe to say that the working class is spontaneously gravitating towards socialism, fed up with capitalism, seeking a logical alternative. It is also safe to say that the capitalists are well aware of this, and are responding by "muddying the waters", spreading as much confusion as they can. As they are well versed in such matters, with years of experience, it is an impressive amount.

One of their favourite tricks is to confuse the economic base of capitalism, with the political super structure, that of the democratic republic. They would have us believe that capitalism is democracy, while socialism is a dictatorship!

In fact, democracy is a form of class rule, that of one class over another class. Under capitalism, it is the rule of the capitalist class, the bourgeoisie, over the working class, the proletariat. This has resulted in a democracy for the insignificant few, the tiny minority of capitalists, over the vast majority of working people, the proletariat. Democracy under capitalism amounts to the dictatorship of the bourgeoisie.

It is a fundamental tenet of Marxism that such a democracy must be replaced by a different type of democracy. The capitalists must be overthrown and crushed by the working class. The existing state apparatus, which has been set up by the capitalists, in order to crush the working people, must be destroyed and replaced by a different state apparatus. This new state apparatus must be set up by the working class, after the revolution, with a view to crushing the capitalists. It is referred to as the Dictatorship Of the Proletariat.

The first example of a successful socialist revolution and the subsequent Dictatorship Of the Proletariat, was that of the October Revolution in Russia, 1917. It was Lenin who led this revolution to victory. This gave rise to the Soviet Union. After the death of Lenin, Stalin carried on and led the country to victory over the Nazis in the Great Patriotic War of 1941-1945.

After the death of Stalin, capitalism was restored in the Soviet Union.

The lesson to be learned from this is that after the revolution, it is absolutely necessary to crush the capitalists, as they are not about to resign themselves to a life of manual labour. That is where the Dictatorship Of the Proletariat comes in. In the Soviet Union, they were not crushed, or at least not with sufficient enthusiasm.

In much the same manner, China became a socialist country in 1949, but after the death of Mao, the capitalists were able to return to power. To this day, the government of China claims to be Marxists, while in fact they are social chauvinists.

The class war will not end with the successful revolution, the overthrow of the capitalists. It will merely move to a different battle field.

Possibly the best way to exercise dictatorship over those parasites is to give the billionaires a job in the countryside, working on a farm, shovelling manure and growing crops. They should be able to handle livestock, such as chicken, hogs and cattle. They may even be able to grow crops such as potatoes, carrots and turnips. While they are kept busy on the farm, it may be best to keep them away from any electronic devices. Given the chance to communicate with other members of their class, they will almost certainly concoct a scheme to cause trouble. That is their nature.

This may sound harsh, but only because it is harsh. Under socialism, we want everyone to be useful. People who are sitting in prison cells all day are of no use to anyone. On the other hand, absolute dictatorship must be maintained at all times. We must not repeat the mistakes of Russia and China, in which the capitalists were not completely crushed.

In preparation for the revolution, which will give rise to the Dictatorship Of the Proletariat, we want to appeal to as many people as possible, providing they are not the enemy. For that reason, we have got to examine the various groups and parties in the country.

The CPUSA, or Communist Party USA, is a very clear cut example of a political party which claims to be Marxist, but is not. I say "clear cut" because they openly admit to being "revisionist". This is to say that they maintain that the revolutionary theories of Marx and Lenin must be revised. They see no need for revolution or the Dictatorship Of the Proletariat. In fact, they see no need for anything which the capitalists may find to be unacceptable. In their opinion, the revolutionary motion should be diverted onto some harmless path of social reform. If nothing else, we give them credit for being openly revisionist.

A less clear cut example is provided by the Communist Party of Canada, Marxist Leninist. Their nine point party platform is as follows:

1. A new direction for the economy that upholds public rights, not monopoly rights.
2. An end to paying the rich and immediately to increase funding for social programs.
3. Renewal of the political process

4. A modern constitution
5. Providing security by defending the rights of all
6. Ending colonial injustice
7. Establishing an anti war government
8. International trade based on mutual benefit and development
9. Solving the problems of environmental destruction and climate change by empowering human beings

Lenin had a few words to say about such people in his article, What Is To Be Done? He referred to them as "Economists", and their political platform is little different from that of the parties which are thought to be very liberal. If anything, these Economists are more devoted to the capitalists. They make every effort to present themselves as leaders of the working class, while trying to divert the revolutionary movement onto some harmless path of social reform.

That is a very clear cut example of a social chauvinist political party. There can be no question of forming an alliance with them, as they are clearly in the service of the capitalists. Other social chauvinist parties are not so transparent.

As that is the case, that begs the question: How are the people who are taking part in the revolution able to distinguish between the Communists and the chauvinists?

May I suggest that the name be that of the American Communist Party, Dictatorship Of the Proletariat, or ACP,DOP. The Dictatorship Of the Proletariat is a fundamental tenet of Marxism, and the worst nightmare of the capitalists. The chauvinists avoid any mention of this, as if it is an infectious disease.

The point is that we can work with the centrists, respecting the differences of each other. We can support them in their struggle for reforms, while at the same time putting forth our revolutionary beliefs. It is not necessary that they share our belief in revolution. It is necessary that they do not oppose the revolution.

We absolutely cannot work with the social chauvinists. They are the enemy. They may or may not admit to being revisionists. It matters not. A clear line must be drawn, between the working class and the capitalist class, and that includes their servants, the social chauvinists.

# CHAPTER 8

# BREXIT, IMPERIALISM AND THE STATE

Lately, the fact that the United Kingdom has voted to break away from the European Union, has captured the attention of all the mainstream news outlets. This has led to considerable confusion among the members of the public, many of whom cannot understand the reason for the uproar, or even the parties involved. We consider it best to clarify matters.

The word Brexit is a combination of the words British and exit. The countries of England, Scotland and Wales, which are located on one rather small island, together are referred to as Great Britain. The people of these countries generally refer to themselves as British.

The addition of Northern Ireland to Great Britain comprises the United Kingdom. It should be noted that at present, the United Kingdom is anything but united.

Now that the citizens have voted to break away from the European Union, the EU, there are a great many who also want to break away from the United Kingdom, the UK. This includes the people of Scotland and Northern Ireland.

It is assumed that if Northern Ireland were to break away from the United Kingdom, it would almost certainly rejoin Ireland, and the country would once again be united. It would also mean the end of the United Kingdom.

Then if Scotland were to break away, Great Britain would be composed of England and Wales. Further, it is not at all clear that Wales is content to remain tied to England. Should Wales choose to cut all ties to England, then that would spell the end of Great Britain.

This has created a great deal of concern, not just in Europe, but also in America. The EU consists of twenty eight countries, the so called United States of Europe. This is a dream come true for the imperialists of Europe, the monopoly capitalists of the so called "Great Powers". This is the class of people who are determined to extract the greatest possible profits from the smaller, less powerful, subordinate countries.

These smaller countries, which are still formally independent, are in fact enmeshed in the net of financial and political dependence, and are basically semi colonial countries.

This is but one example of finance capital being such a great, decisive force in all economic and international relations, that countries may appear to enjoy complete political independence, but are in fact subordinate to countries that are highly developed, the so called Great Powers.

Naturally, imperialists do not refer to this exploitation of smaller countries as semi colonialism, as that would be honest, and no one has ever accused the imperialists of being honest. They refer to this as "free trade".

In fact, this is the age of monopoly capitalism, known by the scientific term of *imperialism*, which is an immense accumulation of capital in a few countries. As a result of this, we have an extremely rich class of bond holders, rentiers, or people who live by "clipping coupons". who take no part whatever in production and whose profession is idleness. They are parasites who live on the exploitation of the labor of the workers of various countries. The scientific term for these parasites, these monopoly capitalists, these billionaires, is *bourgeoisie*.

The fact of the matter is that the political features of imperialism are "reaction all along the line", according to Lenin, and increased national oppression, as a result of the oppression by the financial oligarchy and the elimination of free competition.

Of course, the bourgeois economists do not phrase it in these terms. It is in their interest to gloss over these facts, to present imperialism in the most glowing terms.

In fact, imperialism is the epoch of finance capital and of monopolies, which introduce everywhere the striving for domination, not for freedom. They strive to exploit an ever increasing number of small or weak nations, by an extremely small group of the richest and most powerful nations.

It is against this background that we must examine the Brexit, as it is called.

This vote of the people of the United Kingdom to separate from the European Union, however historic, is merely part of a world wide working class movement, a revolutionary movement, against the monopoly capitalists, the bourgeoisie.

The imperialists must be overthrown, and they will be crushed, but it will not be easy. They are extremely wealthy, and they have every intention of hanging onto that wealth, and even to build upon it. Even though they have more money than they could ever hope to spend, it is not enough. They are constantly trying to squeeze ever more from us, the working people.

As the capitalists are well aware, our differences are deep and antagonistic. That which is in our best interests, is in their worst interests. It is to their advantage to work us as hard as possible, while paying us as little as possible, thereby assuring them the highest possible profit. It also assures us a life of poverty, which is of absolutely no concern to the imperialists. The only way in which this class of parasites can be overthrown is through revolution.

To place this in its proper historical perspective, we can compare this to the country of France, at the time of the French revolution. At that time, it was the nobility who lived in the "lap of luxury", crushing and exploiting the working people, peasants and workers alike. The suffering of the common people was terrible, yet they still managed to rise up and destroy the nobles.

Over the years, the classes have changed and the state apparatus has changed. The determination of the ruling class, in this case the bourgeoisie, to stay in power, remains the same. They are determined to continue to crush and exploit the working class. To that end, they have created a state apparatus, which is composed of the army, police, courts, prisons and various "correctional institutions", all of which are nothing more than an expression of the irreconcilability of class antagonisms.

According to Marx, the state is an organ of class rule – an organ for the oppression of one class by another. It has been set up by the capitalists to keep the working class subjugated.

Now the working people are rising up, challenging the rule of the capitalists. The existing state machine, that was set up by the capitalists to crush the working class, cannot be used against the capitalists. It must be destroyed.

After the revolution, after the capitalists are overthrown, it will be necessary to establish a new state machine. The resistance of the capitalists will be increased ten fold as they strive to restore capitalism, to return to their life of luxury, to their "paradise lost". For that reason, they must be crushed.

This new state machine must be in the form of a new type of democracy -a democracy of the working class, by the working class, for the working class. For the tiny minority of capitalists, those who are determined to return to power, there will be a dictatorship, the Dictatorship Of the Proletariat.

After the successful transition to socialism, all members of the working class must be involved in crushing the capitalists. Of course, leaders are required, chosen from the working class, subject to recall at any time, and paid the wages of workers.

This world wide revolutionary movement is unprecedented. All previous revolutions have been confined to one country or possibly one area of the world. This current revolution has spread around the world, and is very strong and fine. What is more, it is being led by women, those who are well organized, focused and disciplined. It is possible that the ruling capitalists in smaller, freer republican countries may prefer to step aside, without a fight.

Yet in the countries where imperialism is firmly established, there can be no doubt that a peaceful transition to socialism is merely a "pipe dream". The contradictions between the monopoly capitalists and the vast majority of working people, are now sharp and clear. There is no way the billionaires are about to give up without a fight. They have too much to lose. Besides, they are probably afraid of being charged with the numerous crimes they committed while in power.

If the uprising is carefully organized and carried out according to plan, the actual seizure of power may be almost bloodless, as was the case of Russia, October 1917. In that case, the working people had proper leaders, in the form of the Communist Party, although at that time the name was different. In the absence of such leadership, any spontaneous uprising is bound to be disorganized and could result in a blood bath. The point being that the formation of a Communist Party is of vital importance.

Working people are not a bunch of soft hearted, sentimental humanitarians. As the revolution rages, we can expect workers to deal harshly with the mobsters who have brutalized them. It is only in this way that they can break the "invisible chains", to overcome the terror they have, of those human parasites.

In the first American revolution, the "mob" broke down the doors of government officials, dragged those people out into the streets, and coated them with tar and feathers. Such behaviour is normally considered to be inappropriate, but during a revolution, the usual polite rules of civilized society are suspended.

The journalists, or at least those who report for the mainstream press, tend to accurately report that which is happening, but fail to grasp the fact that it is a revolution. Either they cannot imagine a revolution, or are not allowed to state the obvious. But then it is not in their best interests to mention anything of that nature.

It is clear that the capitalists are blissfully unaware of the revolutionary storm, which is about to wash over them.

# CHAPTER 9

# CONCERNING GLOBAL WARMING

ately the news outlets, as well as a certain former vice president, have been preoccupied with climate change, in the form of "global warming". Apparently we, the members of the public, are responsible. At least, that seems to be the message the politicians and scientists are preaching. Shame on us.

They would have us believe that the Industrial Revolution and the subsequent burning of "fossil fuels" have given rise to "greenhouse gasses", which contribute to global warming. They also talk, at great length, about our "carbon footprint" and the necessity of reducing that carbon footprint.

Those are rather serious accusations, and rather confusing. But then it is meant to be confusing. It is also meant to distract working people from the revolutionary motion that is currently sweeping the country, if not the world, and focus our attention on inconsequential matters.

But as people are talking about this, perhaps it is best to clarify matters. We can start by explaining a few terms, starting with *global warming.* This is quite simply a reference to a rise in global temperatures, and is presented as a fact.

It is not at all clear that the world is warming. The evidence presented is quite contradictory, and there are numerous scientists who dispute this. It is clear that the *continent* of North America is in the midst of a warm period, as opposed to an ice age. Within the last hundred thousand years, we have had three ice ages, in which glaciers covered the continent. This is rather recent by geological standards. This in no way implies that warming is happening around the world.

The fact that certain scientists dispute this theory of global warming is encouraging, and shows a certain amount of courage on the part of those people. To express any dissenting opinion is not in their best interests. They are being accused on not being team players. As if science is now a team sport!

The idea of global warming is just a theory, not a fact, and as such, is meant to be challenged. Without a doubt, the climate is always changing – either warming up or cooling down, either becoming dryer or "wetter". Never in the history of the world has the climate remained constant, unchanging. But then there is a reason we have four seasons.

The scientists most graciously explain to us -as if we were a bunch of dummies- that heat from the sun, in the form of solar radiation, warms up the world, and allows life to exist on planet earth. No kidding! They also explain that the atmosphere on this planet, which consists of various gasses, helps to trap some of that solar radiation. Perhaps the most important gas in that respect is carbon dioxide, or $CO_2$, otherwise known as greenhouse gas, and no doubt there is some truth to this.

There is also no doubt that carbon is stored in plants such as trees, as well as fossil fuels, which is to say petroleum, coal and natural gas. But then we dastardly humans release this carbon into the atmosphere when we burn these items. This extra carbon in the atmosphere adds to the $CO_2$, and that gives rise to more greenhouse gasses, which traps more solar radiation, and causes the planet to warm up more quickly. Therefore, global warming is our fault, and we should be ashamed of ourselves. Or so the scientists tell us, and in fact they mention this frequently and at great length.

To proceed, the *carbon footprint* is defined as "the total amount of greenhouse gasses produced to directly or indirectly support human activities, or the total set of greenhouse gas emissions caused by an individual". That is certainly an impressive definition. To say that it lacks clarity is an understatement. In fact, it is a masterpiece of confusion. The individual who came up with that jewel deserves an award as the Confusion Expert of the Year. Give that fellow a raise!

It has even been suggested, by a certain highly respected scientist, that as a result of global warming, we can expect "wild" fluctuations in the weather. No doubt this stands in stark contrast to "tame" fluctuations in the weather. That same scientist is careful not to draw a distinction between "wild fluctuations" in the weather, as opposed to "tame fluctuations".

To say that we can expect "wild fluctuations in the weather", as a result of "global warming", is a safe statement, as there is no way to prove or disprove this theory.

The implication is that we really should be ashamed of ourselves. Instead of heating our houses with propane or wood, we really should shiver in the cold. For that matter, we should quit building houses, as that would save on wood. As well, we really should park our vehicles and quit using electricity, quit reading newspapers and magazines, and return to a Stone Age existence.

Such a life style is certainly appealing, in the sense that it offers the bright, shining virtue of simplicity. It would be quite a change from the rat race to which most of us have become accustomed. There is not a great deal more that can be said for such a drastic change in life, and of course such a suggestion is completely ridiculous. No one in his right mind is about to seriously consider a return to the life style of a nomad- gathering food by hand, hunting with a bow and arrow, eating raw meat and fish- as a simple camp fire requires the burning of wood, and such an act contributes to global warming.

Equally ridiculous is the idea of climate change being caused by people burning wood and coal for heat, driving vehicles and buying newspapers.

Somehow I doubt that our Stone Age ancestors worried about global warming, and they no doubt used fire to stay warm, as well as to cook their meat and vegetables. That was the only way they could possibly have survived. Equally without doubt, they too were subjected to climate change, in the form of the occasional ice age, followed by warming ages, at which time the glaciers melted. Then too, there were droughts as well as floods -both of which can be devastating. If these are not examples of "wild fluctuations in the weather", then I do not know what is!

The fact is that ever since the creation of the world, complete with an atmosphere, the climate has always been changing. There have been occasions when we have had very severe winters, complete with severe cold and heavy snow fall. We have also on occasion had very hot, dry summers, just as we have had cool, wet summers, complete with flooding. This is nothing other than an act of God.

It is safe to say that in different parts of the world, at any particular time, the climate is changing, either becoming warmer and dryer or possibly cooler and wetter. This is not to say that the planet as a whole is warming up or cooling down, although that may well be the case.

Here in North America, it is clear that the climate is becoming warmer, if not dryer, and the glaciers are continuing to melt, or "retreat", as that is the current politically correct term. But then for many thousands of years, the climate here in North America has been warming up, and the glaciers, which formerly covered almost all the continent, have been melting.

This should not cause us any great concern, because as previously mentioned, we have been through three ice ages.

We are merely fortunate to be living at a time of a warm spell, possibly between ice ages.

It should be noted that these warm periods did not take place as a result of greenhouse gasses being released into the atmosphere, or at least not as a result of human interference. In fact, climate change is caused by a number of factors, which include cloud cover, ocean currents, sea levels, solar variability, and volcanic activity, among other things. All of these things are beyond the control of humans. Without a doubt, certain parts of the world, such as North America, are experiencing a warming trend, while other parts of the world appear to be cooling off; still others are getting dryer, others are getting wetter, etc. This has been going on since the creation of the planet, so it should not come as any great shock.

Try telling this to the politicians! They are making countless speeches on the subject, documentaries are being produced, and a few are even writing books on the topic of "global warming".

If our political leaders were really concerned about climate change, as is being caused by the "burning of fossil fuels", then they would encourage the development of alternative sources of energy, such as solar and wind power. People would also be encouraged to grow gardens, start plants in green houses, raise chickens in their back yards, buy crops that are locally grown, and try to become as locally self sufficient as possible.

Such actions would result in an increase in the standard of living of the members of the public, as fresh, healthy food was made available and pollution from vehicles was reduced as a result of fewer vehicles trucking in food from hundreds of kilometres away. But then this is not about to happen, as we live under capitalism.

The capitalists are not concerned with raising the standard of living of the public. They are concerned only with their profit, their "bottom line". The development of agriculture and alternative sources of energy does not concern them, as it would cut into their profit.

The fact is that we live in a class society, and the capitalists are in charge. They are supremely wealthy and own the corporations, banks, railroads, airlines, factories, mills, mines, internet and everything else of any considerable value. The rest of us, who have to work for a living, comprise the working class, technically referred to as the proletariat, but more commonly referred to as "blue collar". We survive as best we can, by working for the capitalists, as there is no choice in the matter. The capitalists make their money off our labour power, so it is in their best interests to pay us as little as possible, while working us as hard as possible. It is in our interests to sell ourselves for the highest possible price. This is another way of saying that our interests are diametrically opposed.

True, we live in a democracy, which is to say that our democratically elected leaders, our members of Parliament, Congress, Senate and such, are devoted to "talk for the special purpose of fooling the common people", according to Marx. That is precisely the reason they are so excited about global warming, so as to divert the attention of the members of the public, the working class, onto a harmless piece of foolishness. In the meantime, the actual decisions are made behind closed doors.

As Marx phrased it, once every few years, the members of the working class get to decide which member of the ruling class gets to misrepresent the people in our various capitals. Once these democratically elected politicians get to the capital, they are encouraged to make speeches to mislead the people they are supposed to represent. This great uproar, concerning global warming, is a fine example of the politicians trying to focus the attention of the working people on an issue that is beyond human control.

The idea is to focus our attention on global warming and divert the current revolutionary movement, one which is sweeping the world. In fact, climate change is an act of God, one which has nothing to do with us. On the other hand, we can certainly strive to clean up our environment, if only by planting gardens and buying locally grown crops, whenever possible.

We can also hold our democratically elected leaders accountable, insist that they quit preaching and start earning their pay. As a start, they may quit wasting tax payer money and perhaps invest it in projects such as solar and wind power.

Aside from that, we have got to face the fact that capitalism is the problem and the whole rotten system has to be abolished. The capitalists, the tiny insignificant minority of billionaires, those who are currently crushing and exploiting us, have to be overthrown and crushed. The current political system of capitalism has to be replaced by socialism. The current rulers have to overthrown and crushed under the iron heel of the proletariat. This is referred to as the Dictatorship Of the Proletariat. It is the one and only way in which the working class can maintain political power, after the revolution.

As the revolution could take place any day now, it is absolutely essential that we prepare for the Dictatorship Of the Proletariat. At the top of the list of those preparations, I would place the creation of a truly Communist Party. That is of the utmost importance.

# CHAPTER 10

# CONCERNING DINOSAUR HERESIES AND MASS EXTINCTIONS

In the world of paleontology, various time periods are neatly divided up and given proper names. In this article, I am mainly concerned with the age of dinosaurs. which the scientists say began with the Triassic Period, proceeded through the Jurassic and the Cretaceous, and ended only with the mass extinction of 65 million years ago, MYA, at the start of the Cenozoic Period. This moment in time is referred to as the K-T boundary, and the paleontologists refer to it as the Great Dying or Great Extinction.

It is their belief that at that time, all dinosaurs and a great many species of reptiles just dropped dead, leaving behind no descendants. This is rather deeply entrenched in the scientific literature, so that it is now almost a sacred belief, which is rather unfortunate, as it is simply not true.

Speaking in general terms, we can say that each time period is characterized by the predominance of certain flora and fauna, in that *flora* refers to the plants, and *fauna* refers to the animals.

To that limited extent, and only to that limited extent, it is useful. To assign definite dates to these time periods is incorrect, as the mass extinction of various species, which generally marks each boundary, is at best questionable. It is more precise to make it clear that one time period blended into another over a period of possibly many millions of years. As conditions changed, species evolved, which gave rise to entirely different species, those which were better able to take advantage of the new environment.

It is also possible that there were mass extinctions of species at various intervals, during the course of history, but this has yet to be proven. In particular, the mass extinction of dinosaurs and reptiles absolutely did not happen.

There is currently considerable confusion concerning dinosaurs, understandably so. Their fossilized remains were not discovered by the scientific community until the early nineteenth century. The scientists of those days were truly puzzled, as at that time, their only reference source was the bible, and in particular, the book of Genesis. That book makes no reference to such large animals, so they were at a loss to explain these monsters. But they did the best they could and decided that these were the remains of huge prehistoric reptiles, which must have lived many years ago. In that spirit, the scientists called them dinosaurs, which means "terrible lizards", as lizards are reptiles.

The choice of names was understandable, but rather unfortunate, as the animals which were classified as "dinosaurs" were not reptiles at all, but birds. We know this for a fact, as they not only laid eggs, they also had feathers. The trouble is that the word *dinosaur* is deeply entrenched in scientific literature, as well as being in popular usage. For that reason, I have chosen to keep using the word, even though it is not accurate. Not that I like it, but there is really no choice in the matter.

Even that statement I have to qualify, as *certain* science books refer to *certain* swimming reptiles, and *all* flying reptiles, as dinosaurs. *All* science books are mistaken, to one degree or another. I maintain that *all* of the land dwelling animals which once walked the earth, and are now referred to as dinosaurs, were in fact birds.

For many years after the earliest paleontologists described these dinosaurs, it was thought that these animals were huge, stupid, sluggish, swamp bound pre historic reptiles, waddling around in the Jurassic swamps. Nothing could be further from the truth. It is to the credit of Dr. Robert Bakker that he dispelled this myth, most notably in his book, The Dinosaur Heresies, first published in 1986.

At the time of its publication, the book received rave reviews. Fellow paleontologists hailed it as "brilliant and authoritative", "spectacular and illustrated", "a real blockbuster", "most enthralling yet understandable", "Bakker explodes old myths,,,soon most of the heresies will be heresies no longer". Now that is high praise!

Such was the opinions of various contemporaries of Bakker, all of whom were well established and respected. The trouble is that while he demolished the old myths and heresies, he merely replaced them with various others. He is absolutely correct when he says that we should be "kind to colleagues, ruthless with theories... A scientific theory is not merely idle speculation, it is a verbal picture of how things might work, how a system in nature might organize things...."

Well spoken! In this, he is absolutely correct. The only trouble is that he does not take his own advice!

It is safe to say that a scientific theory is nothing more than a "glorified idea", one that may, or may not, be correct. This is not to denigrate the value of theory, as it is vitally important to understand how things work. The only way to determine the validity of a theory is to challenge that theory with facts. If the facts contradict the theory, then the theory is to be discarded.

By contrast, the Bakker method is to embrace the theory and either ignore the facts that contradict the theory, or come up with more elaborate theories to explain away these inconvenient facts. Then again, he may present facts that contradict his theory, in an attempt to prove his theory, which makes absolutely no sense. Or he may present other theories as proof that his theories are correct, which makes even less sense.

The mass extinction of dinosaurs is a fine example of one such theory, one that is presented by Bakker as a fact, one that ended in total extinction, a time of Great Dying. He goes so far as to say that "dinosaurs are incontrovertibly dead". We can only assume he used the word *"incontrovertibly"* as a manner of stressing the fact that dinosaurs are dead. Then he goes on to say that *"birds are dinosaurs".* To say that this makes no sense is an understatement, as birds are most emphatically not dead.

He is absolutely correct when he says that birds are dinosaurs. As that is the case, dinosaurs cannot be "incontrovertibly dead". Precisely the opposite. Dinosaurs are "incontrovertibly alive". But then, Bakker is not impressed by logic. It is anathema to the Bakker method.

The fact that dinosaurs are still very much alive in the form of birds is proof that there was no mass extinction of dinosaurs sixty five MYA, but the Bakker method is to disregard facts that disprove his theories.

Of all of the absurdities in his book, and there are a great many, to claim that dinosaurs are dead, while birds are dinosaurs, is perhaps the greatest.

As proof of the theory that dinosaurs suffered a mass extinction sixty five million years ago, he offers no facts, but instead offers the theories of other mass extinctions. He claims the most recent mass extinction was that of "megafauna", which means large animals. It is his belief that no less than five species of huge mammals went extinct -dropped dead- because they were incapable of handling climate change. He, and other scientists, maintain that this happened ten thousand years ago, at the end of the last ice age. They conveniently overlook the fact that those animals *survived three ice ages!*

The only way those animals could possibly have survived those ice ages, was by adapting to climate change. Each time the climate changed, those animals survived. The fact that they were alive at the end of the *third* ice age, proves that, beyond any shadow of a doubt.

One of those huge species is that of the largest canine in the world, the dire wolf. Even the scientists admit the dire wolf still exists, even though they still maintain that the *dire wolf is extinct!* They refer to this as an example of a *"remnant population of an extinct species!*

I refer to this as an "alternative fact", which is nothing other than a bare faced lie. They are supremely well aware that as long as one member of a species is alive, the species is not extinct.

I would also draw the attention of the scientists to another species, the Jefferson ground sloth, named in honour of the third American president. It was clearly alive at the time of Jefferson, so without doubt, it is still alive.

This brings us to the huge cat located within the city of Milwaukee. That is a sabre toothed cat. As only the males of the species have sabre teeth, and this cat is a female, that explains the lack of huge teeth.

It is clear that these species of "megafauna" are very much alive. That particular theory is clearly bogus, so of course Bakker embraces it. In fact, he offers that theory, of one mass extinction, as proof of another mass extinction, that of dinosaurs, even though "birds are dinosaurs". But then the Bakker method is to decree a theory to be correct, and to disregard all facts to the contrary.

To return to his book, it is rather strange that Bakker includes pterosaurs, commonly called pterodactyls, as dinosaurs. The reason I say this, is because Bakker made the point that dinosaurs were "active, intelligent, warm blooded animals". In this he is absolutely correct. Yet pterosaur are reptiles, and reptiles are *not active, intelligent, warm blooded animals!*" For that reason, pterosaurs cannot be dinosaurs!

To proceed. He says on the subject of swimming reptiles: "As dinosaurs were snuffed out at the end of the Cretaceous, the great sea lizards, and the snake necked plesiosaurs were also dying out." Bakker makes no attempt to explain this. He merely states it, as if we should accept his word as proof. Fat chance!

On the other hand, he is correct when he says that "families of cold blooded genera are almost indestructible, because their slow rate of change implies that only very rarely will all the genera in one family become extinct". Here again he flatly contradicted himself! The very swimming reptiles he insists are extinct, cannot possibly be extinct! This is one more example of the Bakker method, which is to accept a theory, and disregard any evidence to the contrary.

Sadly, the Bakker method has been adopted by the scientific community. His method is to be "kind to theories", ruthless with facts! It is clear that his contemporaries have embraced the Bakker method. The kindest thing that can be said, is that this method is completely non professional. In fact, it makes a mockery of the scientific method.

Yet Bakker is clearly convinced that the mass extinction of dinosaurs actually happened, all evidence to the contrary be damned! Numerous theories have been put forward to explain this mass extinction, and he lists several of them. He also makes the point that all of these theories are ridiculous, which is true. Then he states his own theory to explain that mass extinction. By contrast, his theory is more elaborate, but equally ridiculous.

The Bakker theory is that the mass extinction of dinosaurs was brought about as a result of "continental drift", which brought various species and diseases together. The objection that the continents were quite well separated by vast oceans sixty five million years ago, much as they are today, he has covered. His response is that the oceans, at that time, were "shallow". The word "shallow" is open to interpretation. He takes it to mean that diseases and species crossed these oceans! Not likely!

Bakker is convinced that dinosaurs went extinct because they were warm blooded animals. He conveniently overlooks the fact that mammals are also warm blooded animals, and did not go extinct. In fact, there are more holes in his theory than in a sieve.

To plow through his massive tome is by no means a pleasant task. There is no point in trying to make sense of what he is saying, because he makes no sense. He is under the impression that it is sufficient to declare something to be correct. This is similar to a king who makes a decree. If different decrees contradict each other, that is of no concern to the king.

In all fairness to Bakker, he succeeded in demolishing the "heretical belief" that dinosaurs were stupid reptiles, blundering around in the swamps. It is true that they were "active, intelligent, warm blooded animals". In the year 1986, this was a revelation, long over due. This is to his credit.

On the other hand, Bakker has perpetuated several heresies, such as the mass extinction of dinosaurs, as well as reptiles, both flying and swimming, and mega fauna.

On balance, we can say that the heresies and confusion he has created have done more damage to science, than any heresies he has debunked.

The fact is that the flying reptiles are very much alive, nocturnal animals which are preying upon people and livestock. The members of the public are blissfully unaware of the existence of either the flying or swimming reptiles. This has resulted in the disappearance of countless people, which persists to this day.

No doubt, there are a great many scientists who are aware of the existence of these animals. but are afraid to speak out, for fear of losing their careers.

The question that naturally arises is just how such a book of science, complete with such glaring blunders, could be greeted with rave reviews by fellow scientists.

We can only conclude that the scientists are members of their very own mutual admiration society, and any criticism of each other and their theories is strictly forbidden. This is their idea of being "kind to colleagues". As I am not a colleague, this rule does not apply to me. Further, as I do not have a career, I cannot be threatened with "career suicide". In fact, I committed career suicide many years ago. But then, my conscience is clear.

Those who are successful in any field of science are well aware that to challenge any scientific theory, regardless of the absurdity of the theory, is to commit career suicide. Those of us who are failures in science, which is to say those of us who challenge scientific theories, can testify to that fact. We are not allowed to earn a living, working in any field of science.

As I have devoted my life to challenging scientific theories, I speak from experience. Not that I refer to them as scientific theories, but as scientific "fairy tales". This fails to endear me to the scientific community. I am doing this as a sideline, not getting paid for it, working at it in my spare time. I am not part of the scientific hypocrisy. There is a price to be paid for maintaining a clear conscience.

Many years ago, I was told that I was a trouble maker, rocking the boat, and that I do not belong. In this, my critics were correct. I freely admit that I was a trouble maker, rocking the boat, and did not belong. Those days are long gone, and now I am back, still a trouble maker but no longer rocking the boat. Now I am blowing the boat right out of the water!

As a result of this blind acceptance of theories, science has been reduced to a farce. People in positions of authority are putting forth various harebrained ideas, and worse, such nonsense is being taught in schools.

As for those who think that this is not a serious problem, I can only respond with a reference to the "good old days", when everyone knew that the earth was flat and further, that we live at the centre of the universe. Of course, nothing could be farther from the truth, but it must have been nice to live in a world of such simplicity.

Sadly, the state of science today is little different. The scientists of today, or at least those who are highly respected, are putting forth theories that are nonsense. Worse, such theories are not to be challenged. Any other scientist who dares challenge such theories commits career suicide. So they remain silent, rather than doing their duty. They prefer to play it safe.

This in no way changes the fact that they are responsible for their actions, or lack thereof. To choose to remain silent concerning the continued existence of the mega fauna is inexcusable. Further, to continue to deny the existence of the pterosaur, the animal which kills more people than all other wild animals put together, is possibly criminally negligent. The same is true of the swimming reptiles, also man eaters. And let us not forget gigantopithecus, the largest ape in the world, twice the size of gorillas, one that lives among us, here and now, in North America. Further, it is nothing less than a separate species of human.

That particular species is commonly referred to as Sasquatch or Bigfoot, although I refer to them as Giants, and are in desperate need of protection. The scientists are careful to ignore or even deny all evidence of those people, so now members of our species are determined to murder one of them, as a means to prove they exist.

That is of course merely a partial list, and if nothing else, it must be said that we are entitled to our wild life. It is part of our heritage. Africa and Asia have their elephants, while we have our woolly mammoths. Africa has lions, Asia has tigers, while we have the sabre toothed cat. We do not have gorillas or orangutans, but we do have Giants, the largest ape in the world, and human.

The scientists and politicians are denying us our heritage and lying to us. They have to be held accountable.